CW00967756

THE
PEAK DISTRICT

CONTENTS

MYRIAD
LONDON

Buxton

This elegant town retains many of the splendid buildings from its period as a fashionable spa.

Buxton lies in a hollow surrounded by hills on all sides. Here limestone and gritstone meet, allowing for the creation of the thermal springs that have long been the source of its fortunes. Since Roman times Buxton has been a place of pilgrimage for those seeking cures for their ills, but it was not until the late 18th century that the town came into its own as a fashionable spa. The Old Hall Hotel (above) is reputed to be the oldest hotel in England. It occupies the site of the former townhouse of Bess of Hardwick and her husband the Earl of Shrewsbury. Mary Queen of Scots was held here as a "house prisoner" in 1573. The Town Hall (left), built in 1889, is in the Higher Town – Buxton's original town centre.

BUXTON ATTRACTIONS Dating
from 1903, the magnificent Opera House
(above) in The Square was designed by
Frank Matcham, one of Britain's finest
theatre architects. It now hosts the town's
famous annual music festivals – including
the opera festival in mid-July and the
Gilbert & Sullivan Festival. The Devonshire Royal Hospital (right) in Devonshire
Road boasts the largest unsupported
dome in the country – larger even than
that of St Paul's in London. Originally
a stables for the horses of spa visitors,
the building was converted into a hospital
in 1881, when the dome was added. It is
now part of the University of Derby. The
pedestrianised Spring Gardens (top right)
is Buxton's main shopping street.

SPA FEVER The 5th Duke of Devonshire, a descendant of Bess of Hardwick, was determined that Buxton should rival Bath in its magnificence. Flush with money from his many local coppermines, in the late 1770s he commissioned John Carr of York to build the Crescent (previous page) next to the famous spring of St Ann's Well.

This magnificent street was intended to rival the Royal Crescent at Bath. Constructed from the local gritstone, the Crescent, which had 42 pilasters and 378 windows, included a ballroom, an Assembly Room and a town-house for the Duke. The Duke subsequently built the Great Stable, Hall Bank and the Square all in the same imposing style. By the time of the arrival of the railway in 1863 Buxton was at the height of its popularity. The Pump Room (right), facing the Crescent, was built in 1894; it is the building to which visitors flocked to "take the waters". It is still possible to sample the spa water at the nearby public fountain at St Ann's Well.

PAVILION GARDENS At the heart of Buxton are the Pavilion Gardens, a beautiful 23 acre site designed in 1871 by landscape gardener Edward Milner. Milner had worked with Joseph Paxton on the re-siting of the Crystal Palace from Hyde Park to Sydenham following the Great Exhibition of 1851. The Gardens are home to the impressive concert hall known as the Octagon (above) and the famous Edwardian opera house. Adjoining the Octagon is the Paxton Suite (right) which was added to the side of the Octagon in 1889. This space is now used as a restaurant and exhibition hall.

VICTORIAN SPLENDOUR
The beautiful gardens which surround the Conservatory and Octagon were laid out in 1871 by Edward Milner with money donated by the Dukes of Devonshire. Their 23 acres include formal gardens, a miniature railway and serpentine walks along the banks of the Wye. The bandstand (right) was opened in 1997. In 2004 the gardens were restored to their original splendour and are now visited by more than half a million people every year. One of the highlights, in the often cool climate of the Peak District, is a visit to the hothouse, home to numerous tropical and subtropical plants. Every May the Pavilion Gardens host the annual Buxton antiques fair.

Central Peak Villages

Many of the area's prettiest villages are to be found in the heart of the Peaks.

Ashford-in-the-Water, two miles north-west of Bakewell on the river Wye, is a surprisingly quiet and idyllic village despite its proximity to its larger neighbour. Although lead was mined in the area until the late 19th century, Ashford is most famous for the so-called Black Marble, an impure form of limestone which turns black when polished. First quarried in 1748 by Henry Watson, it was much loved by the Victorians who used it when making fireplaces, vases and jewellery. It was also perfect for mosaic and inlaid patterns.

ASHFORD ATTRACTIONS Some fine examples of black marble can be seen in the great limestone church of the Holy Trinity (left). Largely rebuilt in 1871, the base of the church tower dates from the 13th century. The church has a fine black marble table as well as a plaque to the memory of Henry Watson, the founder of the local marble works. The beautiful stained-glass windows are by William Morris and Edward Burne-Jones. Many of the stone cottages in the village served as workshops for production of black marble before Watson established his factory.

HASSOP Three miles north of the market town of Bakewell, the tiny village of Hassop grew up around the local leadmining industry which proliferated until the mid 19th century. The imposing Hassop Hall (below) was rebuilt in its current form in the early 17th century on the site of a much older house owned by the Eyre family, whose wealth came from leadmining. An old leadmine still exists under the house beneath a manhole hidden in the cellar. The Eyres were devout Catholics; during the Civil War in 1643, the hall was established as a Royalist garrison by Roland Eyre. Several skirmishes took place nearby; following the Parliamentary victory, the captured hall was redeemed by the family who paid £21,000 for the privilege – a massive sum at the time. The church of All Saints (right) was designed as a private chapel for the Eyre family in the Classical style by the Catholic architect Joseph Ireland in 1818. It is connected to the hall by an underground passage. The church is in the style of a classical temple and has an impressive portico and barrel-vaulted interior. Hassop Hall is now an elegant hotel and a popular venue for weddings. Hassop Station, to the south of the village, was built in 1863 to serve the Duke of Devonshire at Chatsworth House.

GREAT LONGSTONE The twin villages of Great and Little Longstone sit beneath Longstone Edge just east of Hassop. Longstone Edge is now disfigured by the lead workings which brought the village its early prosperity. The medieval cross (left) dates even further back to the time when Great Longstone had a flourishing weaving and shoemaking industry, whose patron saint Crispin is commemorated in the adjacent Crispin Inn. Flowers now bloom in the trough (right) below the last of the two village water pumps. St Giles' church (above), hidden away at the end of the village, dates back to the end of the 13th century. Inside there is a memorial to Dr Edward Buxton who, in the early part of the 19th century, tended the village during an outbreak of typhus.

LITTON The 17th and 18th century stone cottages of Litton are clustered around the village green with its stocks and ancient cross. Litton flourished as a centre of stocking-making in the 18th century; Litton Mill, built in 1762, is now a ruin and stands as a monument to the many orphans who toiled there in appalling conditions. Unlike the mill at nearby Cressbrook, Litton Mill was notorious for the poor treatment of its young workforce, largely made up of orphans and paupers. The Red Lion pub (above) is a popular destination for the many visitors who flock to the village in the summer.

TIDESWELL A few miles north-west of Litton, on the river Wye, Tideswell is one of the Peak District's most ancient settlements. It dates back to pre-Roman times and was granted its market charter in 1251. The prosperity of Tideswell was founded on leadmining; in the 19th century it became a centre for the textile industry, producing both cotton and silk goods. Tideswell's magnificent 14th century church of St John the Baptist (right) is often called "the Cathedral of the Peak" and is a testament to the wealth of the area in the Middle Ages. The church was built by Sir John Foljambe, a member of the well-known Derbyshire landowning family, and has a beautiful high nave and outstanding wooden carvings by the Hunstones, local woodcarvers.

CHELMORTON Four miles south-east of Buxton, the village of Chelmorton is 1200ft (366m) above sea level, the highest in Derbyshire. The steep hill of Chelmorton Low looms above the village from which a stream flows down bearing the name of Illy Willy Water. Parts of the church of St John the Baptist (right) date back to Norman times, although the spire was added to the tower in the 15th century. Chelmorton retains many medieval strip farms in the fields around the village, and some of the 13 surviving strips are visible in the photograph above. Most strip farming of this type has long since disappeared to make way for modern agriculture with its much larger fields. However, the land in Chelmorton was considered to be of such poor quality that the medieval field pattern remained untouched to this day.

SHELDON A stone's throw from Bakewell, Sheldon was once the centre of a thriving leadmining industry where rival gangs competed ruthlessly for the best veins of ore: today it is a sleepy village of stone cottages and farms. The Magpie Mine (right), half a mile south of the village, is one of the best preserved leadmines in Britain and features a distinctive Cornish-style engine house and chimney. The mine operated for 300 years but finally closed in 1924. It was the scene of the notorious Magpie Murders in 1833 when three miners were killed by fires started deliberately in a dispute over ownership of a rich vein of lead ore. Rumour has it that the widows of the dead men cursed the mine and that the ghosts of the miners haunt the old workings to this day. Like Ashford-in-the-Water, black marble was mined here, but the mine-workings at Sheldon were hampered by a lack of the large quantities of water needed to polish the stone. The village consists of a single row of stone cottages. They mostly date back to the 18th century when leadmining was at its peak. The church of St Michael and All Angels (right) was built in the 19th century.

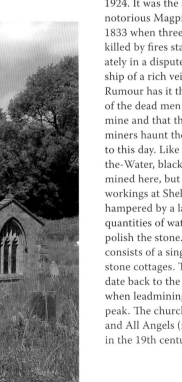

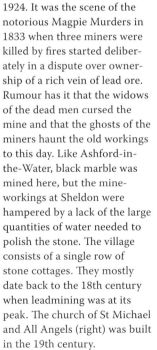

MONYASH Situated near the head of Lathkill Dale, the little village of Monyash clusters around its village green. This ancient farming village is sited on a bed of impervious clay which originally held five stretches of water known as "meres", fed by underground springs. Just one remains – Fere Mere (right) which was once the source of the village's water supply. As the centre for leadmining in the White Peak, Monyash held a Barmote court which sat twice a year to settle mining disputes. Monyash received its market charter in 1340 and the old market cross still stands on the village green. The 12th-century church of St Leonard (right) has interesting priest seats made of stone in the chancel.

OVER HADDON The hamlet of Over Haddon (below) sits at the top of the hill, giving beautiful views across Lathkill Dale. The river which gives the dale its name rises just below Monyash and flows down to meet the Wye below Haddon Hall. In its first stretch it is no more than a dry river bed until it reaches Lathkill House Cave where a spring emerges during wet weather. This section of the valley was once home to several lead-mines. Remains of the Mandale Mine – the most important of the leadmines – can be found at the junction of the Mandale valley and Lathkill Dale. Sections of the workings can still be clearly seen; they include the aqueduct which carried water to a large wheel used to pump water from the mine.

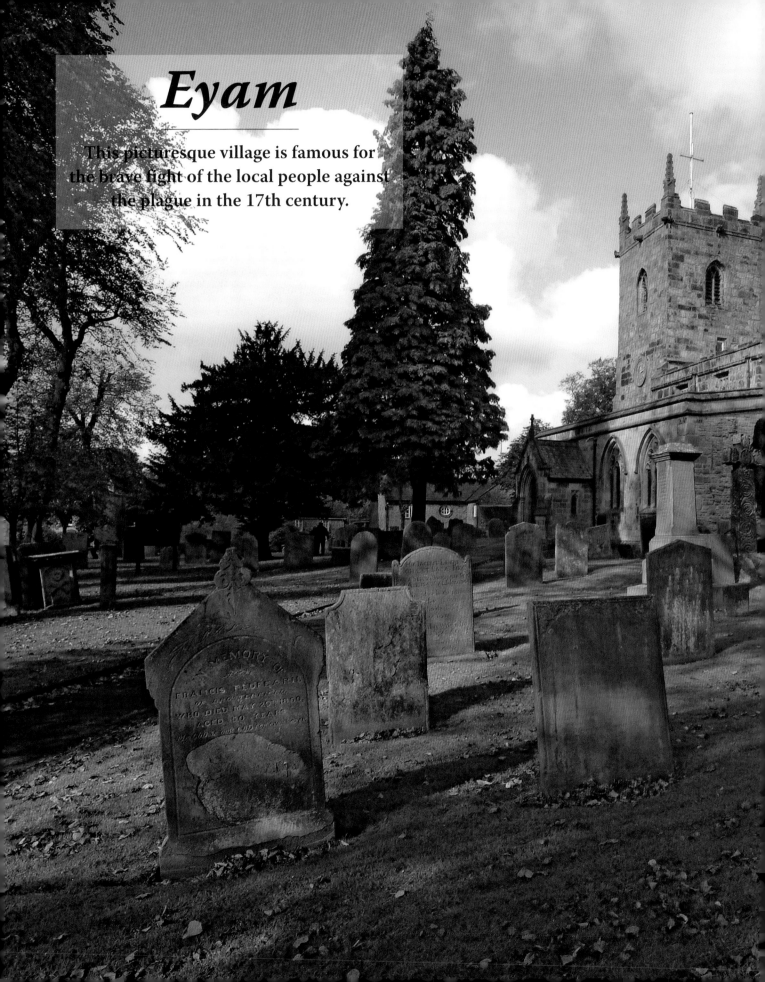

Eyam

This picturesque village is famous for the brave fight of the local people against the plague in the 17th century.

Eyam is known as "the plague village", a reference to the time in 1665 when the inhabitants went into quarantine in order to prevent the plague – which had reached them – spreading to neighbouring villages. The disease first appeared in Eyam in the house now known as the Plague Cottage, then occupied by a travelling tailor who inadvertently carried the plague from London in a parcel of flea-infested cloth. William Mompesson, the rector, persuaded most of the inhabitants to stay and seal off the village even though many later died from the disease. The church of St Lawrence (left) contains artefacts dating back to the period including Mompesson's chair; the churchyard is the resting place for many of the victims, including Mompesson's wife Catherine. Eyam Hall (below) is a 17th century manor house, home of the Wright family.

Monsal & Miller's Dales

In the 19th century, this beautiful area was thought to have been ruined by the arrival of the railway. Now it is one of the most highly regarded spots in the Peaks.

The reaction of the critic and campaigner John Ruskin to the construction of the Midland Railway viaduct across the valley of the river Wye at Monsal Dale was to declare: "The valley is gone – and now every fool in Buxton can be in Bakewell in half an hour and every fool at Bakewell in Buxton!" The Dukes of Devonshire and Rutland were also opposed to the building of the line since it came too close for comfort to their estates. Modern-day reactions are quite different and the views of the river winding through Upperdale from Monsal Head and from the viaduct itself are now regarded as some of the most beautiful and popular vistas in the Peak District. A number of weirs along the river's length add to the delights of walkers following the nine-mile Monsal Trail.

UPPERDALE Close to Monsal Head, the tiny hamlet of Upperdale lies amidst some of the finest limestone scenery in the Peak District. The river Wye winds through Chee Dale and Miller's Dale before passing beneath Upperdale bridge (above) near the village. This stretch of the river is owned by the Chatsworth Estate and is famous for a unique variety of rainbow trout as well as the more common brown trout. The water around Upperdale is particularly clear because it is filtered through the limestone and so it is easy to spot fish in the river. The Wye is one of three Derbyshire rivers that rise on Axe Edge Moor above Buxton; the others are the Manifold and the Dove. The Wye meets the Derwent at Rowsley and flows through Matlock before joining the river Trent in Nottinghamshire.

MILLER'S DALE The river Wye runs through Miller's Dale and was the source of power for Litton and Cressbrook Mills. The river negotiates a barrage of natural obstacles with mill races and weirs where the power of the water was diverted to drive the mill wheels and other machinery. The glory days of Miller's Dale are associated with the local railway junction where passengers heading to and from Buxton made their connections between London and Manchester on the old Midland Railway. In 1964 the line closed leaving the area to sink into obscurity. Today the station (above left) has been absorbed into the Monsal Trail which runs the length of the valley. One route takes walkers down the platform and onto the cinder path on top of the former track-bed. Approximately 200 yards further on, immediately after the railway bridge, is the disused limekiln (left). Another larger and more modern kiln lies to the west of the station. These furnaces produced the lime used in the construction of many of the buildings of the area.

CRESSBROOK The lofty crag of Peter's Stone (above) stands guard over Cressbrook Dale, a beautiful limestone dale north of the village of Cressbrook. This village, once the site of an important and busy mill, is now a quiet backwater on the river Wye. Cressbrook Mill (left) has been converted into apartments after lying derelict for many years. It was built in 1815 by William Newton, on the site of the original mill owned by Richard Arkwright and his son. Newton was known as "the minstrel of the Peak" and was the author of many local ballads and church hymns. The attractive cottages at the top of the hill were built in the 19th century as good quality accommodation for the millworkers.

Chatsworth

Often called "the Palace of the Peak", Chatsworth is one of the most magnificent stately homes in Britain.

Chatsworth is largely the creation of the first Duke of Devonshire. Between 1686 and 1707, he re-modelled the original house – built by the truly formidable Bess of Hardwick and her second husband William Cavendish – and turned it into a fabulous Palladian mansion. In the years between 1569 and 1584 Mary Queen of Scots was held prisoner at Chatsworth and some of the rooms are still known as the Queen of Scots apartments. Chatsworth is a treasure house of art and antiques; its superb setting was achieved by the 18th century gardener Lancelot "Capability" Brown who swept away the formal gardens and created today's open, natural-looking landscape. The best view of the main facade of the house is from the banks of the river Derwent or from the old bridge.

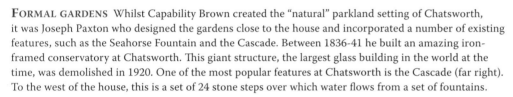

FORMAL GARDENS Whilst Capability Brown created the "natural" parkland setting of Chatsworth, it was Joseph Paxton who designed the gardens close to the house and incorporated a number of existing features, such as the Seahorse Fountain and the Cascade. Between 1836-41 he built an amazing iron-framed conservatory at Chatsworth. This giant structure, the largest glass building in the world at the time, was demolished in 1920. One of the most popular features at Chatsworth is the Cascade (far right). To the west of the house, this is a set of 24 stone steps over which water flows from a set of fountains.

Chatsworth Villages

Beeley and Edensor are two of a handful of pretty villages on the Chatsworth Estate.

BEELEY Six miles north of Matlock, the Chatsworth estate village of Beeley is a small collection of honey-coloured cottages housing estate workers. The village and surrounding countryside were purchased by the Duke of Devonshire in 1747 as part of a grand plan to landscape the estate. The church of St Anne (left) dates back to the 14th century, although much of the existing building is a result of Victorian restoration. The Old Smithy shop and tea rooms (right) provide a welcome refreshment stop for visitors.

PEAK RAIL A train (left) steams through Darley Dale, just south of Beeley, one of the stations on the Peak Rail. The Peak Railway Society run regular steam and diesel trains between Matlock Riverside and Rowsley, part of the old Midland Railway which closed in 1968.

EDENSOR The small village of Edensor (pronounced "Ensor") is set within the beautiful parkland of the Chatsworth Estate. The village was re-located by the 4th Duke of Devonshire so that it would not be seen from Chatsworth House. St Peter's church (below) was designed by the great Victorian church architect Sir George Gilbert Scott, and Joseph Paxton, the 6th Duke's head gardener, is buried in the churchyard.

ROWSLEY Just south of the Chatsworth Estate, at the confluence of the rivers Wye and Derwent, Rowsley is a village of two halves: Greater Rowsley, the original settlement, positioned at the river junction, and Little Rowsley, which developed as a result of the Midland Railway in 1849. Caudwell Mill (above), now a Grade II listed building, was built in 1874. It is the last remaining water turbine-powered flour mill in the country. The mill ran as a family business until it closed in 1978. It is now open to the public every day and visitors can explore the four-storey building and see the machinery in operation. The mellow stone-built Peacock Hotel (below) was built in 1652 by John Stevenson and is now a luxury hotel. A ceramic peacock perches haughtily on the balustrade above the signboard – the emblem of the Manners family, owners of nearby Haddon Hall and proprietors of the Peacock Hotel.

BASLOW North of the Chatsworth Estate on the river Derwent the village of Baslow is divided into three distinct parts: Over End, Nether End and Bridge End. Just up the Derwent, at nearby Calver, the seven-storey former mill (left), which dates back to the 18th century, has been converted into apartments. In the 1970s it was used as the setting for Colditz Castle in the BBC television series *Colditz*.

Bakewell

A busy market town and unofficial capital of the eastern Peaks.

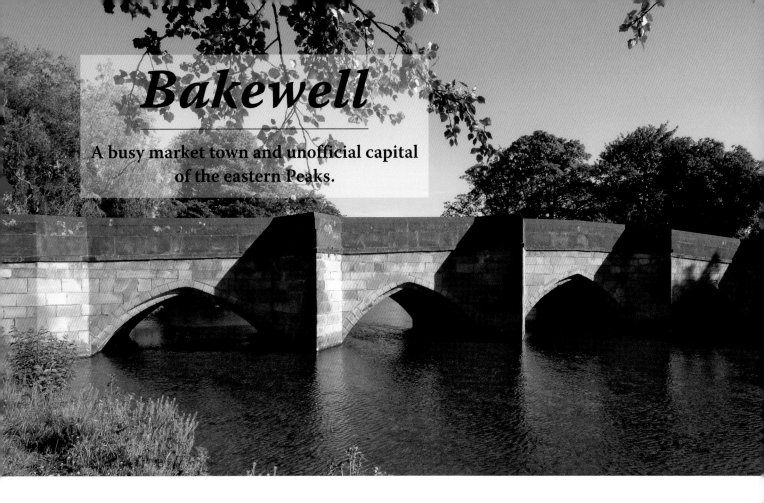

The historic Holme Bridge (above and top right) dates from 1664 and spans the river Wye. Originally a packhorse bridge, it was built here close to a ford which had long been used as a river crossing by wool drovers and merchants. The view west from the bridge (far right) takes in the rippling waters of the river. The famous Bakewell pudding, and its close cousin the Bakewell tart, originated in this little town.

BAKEWELL'S HISTORY The building (above) which houses the Old House Museum once provided accommodation for workers at Sir Richard Arkwright's mill. Close to the museum, on a grassy knoll, sits the imposing Norman church of All Saints (far right). It contains a famous monument to Sir John Manners and his wife Dorothy of nearby Haddon Hall. In the early 19th century the Duke of Rutland, one of whose country seats was at the nearby Haddon Hall, rebuilt Bakewell in an attempt to rival the spa at Buxton established by the Duke of Devonshire. He realigned the streets on a grid pattern which converged on a square just below the Old Town Hall and replaced many timber-framed buildings with beautiful stone houses.

BAKEWELL'S ARCHITECTURE The town is full of mellow stone buildings, many of which date from the 18th century. The Old Town Hall is now a national park information centre and the Bath House is a remnant of Bakewell's former life as a spa town. There are many cottages which were constructed for mill-workers. Lumford Cottages (far left) stand close to Lumford Mill, originally built as a cotton-spinning mill in 1778 by Sir Richard Arkwright.

Haddon Hall

Home of the Dukes of Rutland, Haddon Hall is one of the finest medieval and Tudor houses in England.

The romantic and mysterious Haddon Hall is situated next to the river Wye just south of Bakewell. It is one of the finest medieval and Tudor houses in England and has been the home of the Manners family, the Dukes of Rutland, since 1567. The house changed little over the centuries until, in the 1920s, the 9th Duke of Rutland began a programme of restoration. The air of romance that lingers around the house is in part due to the legend that in 1558 Lady Dorothy Vernon eloped from the house on horseback with Sir John Manners. This inspired the 1927 film *Dorothy Vernon of Haddon Hall*, starring Mary Pickford.

HADDON GARDENS The gardens at Haddon Hall are thought by many to be the most romantic in England. The 9th Duke created the walled topiary garden which adjoins the stable block cottage. It contains many shaped hedges which depict the boar's head and peacock – symbols of the Vernon and Manners families. The terraced rose gardens cascade down the hillside from the curtain wall towards the river. They are planned for colour and scent throughout the summer and climbing roses tumble from the walls, down the balustrades and steps. From each terrace are views across the water meadows and Derbyshire countryside. The hall and gardens have been used as a backdrop for many feature films and television series including *Jane Eyre* and *Moll Flanders*.

Curbar & Baslow Edge

This dramatic two mile long ridge or edge overlooks the villages of Curbar and Calver.

The imposing edges fringing the Peak District are at their most spectacular north of Bakewell where Froggatt's Edge, Curbar Edge and Baslow Edge join in a breathtaking sequence which runs north to south and overlooks the valley of the river Derwent and the villages of Curbar and Calver. The photograph (above) is the view south from Curbar Edge up the Derwent valley; the photograph (right) is one of the imposing cliff faces of Baslow Edge. Behind the edges the landscape becomes an elevated plateau. This bleak spot has clearly been a site of human settlement since the Bronze Age. The surface of the plateau is dotted with cairns and at least one stone circle adjacent to Froggatt's Edge. Nearby, Cundy Graves was a burial place for plague victims.

Eastern Peak Villages

The rocky outcrops of the east Peaks are home to many communities who once made their living by quarrying and mining.

The landscape around Middleton and Wirksworth still bears the scars of lead-mining and limestone quarrying. Walkers on the High Peak Trail, which follows the route of the now abandoned Cromford and High Peak Railway, come across evidence of sidings, engine houses, shafts and quarries. One of the most substantial of the abandoned limestone quarries is at Middleton (right), just to the west of the village. This vast quarry is a reminder of the time when limestone quarrying was a huge industry in this area, helped by the arrival of the railway in nearby Wirksworth in 1867. The National Stone Centre opened in 1990 on the site of a local disused quarry. It tells the story of how the stone was extracted and its economic and social impact on the Peak District.

MIDDLETON The small village of Middleton by Wirksworth is surrounded by extensive quarries and spectacular rock and cliff-faces. Nearby is Middleton Top (below right) with its engine house which was used to haul wagons up the incline on the Cromford and High Peak Railway. A lane in nearby Middleton-by-Youlgreave leads to the tiny church of St Michael (below).

YOULGRAVE Situated on the banks of the river Bradford, Youlgrave boasts an unusual circular tank (right) known as The Fountain. It was once used as a storage tank for water pumped from the river. The 13th century All Saints church (above) is considered second only in importance to the church of St John the Baptist at Tideswell. Its Perpendicular tower can be seen from all over the village. Just around the corner from tiny Thimble Hall are the twin cottages of Tweedledee and Tweedledum (left). Tweedledee is 300 years old, while Tweedleedum is a mere stripling at 200 years.

STANTON-IN-THE-PEAK This attractive village lies along a steep twisting lane below the mysterious Stanton Moor where the Nine Ladies Stone Circle and other prehistoric sites abound. Stanton's glorious architecture is largely the legacy of the Thornhill family who lived at nearby Stanton Hall. There are clear links too with the nearby Chatsworth Estate – the Flying Childers Inn (above left) is named after a racehorse owned by the Duke of Devonshire in the 1700s. This famous horse was never beaten and his portrait hangs at Chatsworth where he died, aged 26, in 1741. The elegant Holly House (above) dates from the 1700s. Two of its windows were blocked up as a result of the window tax of 1697.

ALPORT The picturesque hamlet of Alport is situated three miles south of Bakewell at a dreamy spot where the Bradford and Lathkill rivers meet. Water power played a major part in Alport's development, and there is evidence of a cornmill and a fulling mill in the village in the Middle Ages. In the 18th and 19th centuries this was an industrial settlement with leadmines, a lead smelting mill, a paper mill and weaving, dyeing and bleaching sheds which were used in the wool industry. The magnificent 18th century cornmill which stands on the east bank of the river is a testament to Alport's industrial heritage.

NOTICE TO ALL VAGABONDS FOUND LODGING, LOITERING OR BEGGING WITHIN THIS HAMLET WILL BE TAKEN UP AND DEALT WITH AS THE LAW DIRECTS

ALPORT'S RIVERS On the eastern edge of the Peak District National Park, Alport is a typical limestone village. The river Lathkill descends through the village in a series of picturesque cascades (left) before joining the river Wye which empties into the Derwent at nearby Rowsley. In the 1880s the river Bradford disappeared underground for several years, following the path of an underground drainage canal built to prevent water flooding the many lead-mines in the area. In 1750 a bridge was built at a point where the walking trails to both Bradford Dale and Lathkill Dale now meet. During the summer the area around the bridge is thronged with walkers and hikers enjoying some of the best walks in Derbyshire. The path up the river Bradford to Youl-grave is particularly popular.

Matlock

The heyday of Matlock and Matlock Bath was the Victorian era, when they were fashionable spa resorts.

Matlock is the county town of Derbyshire. It was a collection of small villages until the discovery of warm springs in 1698. John Smedley, the pioneer of hydrotherapy, built the vast hydro in 1853 and another 20 hydros soon followed. Smedley's Hydro (the large building in the photograph, right) is now the offices of Derbyshire County Council. Matlock Bath is situated in a wooded gorge on the river Derwent, a mile to the south. The cable car (left) carries visitors up the 450ft (137m) incline to the Heights of Abraham giving magnificent views. The name is derived from the site of General Wolfe's victory at Quebec in 1759; it was chosen because the gorge was said to resemble that of the great St Lawrence river in Canada. On the opposite side of the valley are the High Tor Grounds, 60 acres of nature trails which climb above the river. From the top, the river Derwent looks like a silver thread winding through the wooded valley bottom.

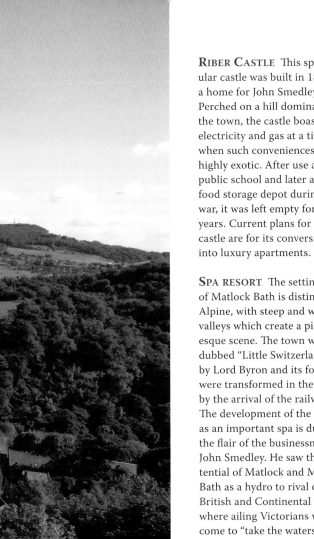

RIBER CASTLE This spectacular castle was built in 1862 as a home for John Smedley. Perched on a hill dominating the town, the castle boasted electricity and gas at a time when such conveniences were highly exotic. After use as a public school and later as a food storage depot during the war, it was left empty for many years. Current plans for the castle are for its conversion into luxury apartments.

SPA RESORT The setting of Matlock Bath is distinctly Alpine, with steep and wooded valleys which create a picturesque scene. The town was dubbed "Little Switzerland" by Lord Byron and its fortunes were transformed in the 1840s by the arrival of the railway. The development of the area as an important spa is due to the flair of the businessman John Smedley. He saw the potential of Matlock and Matlock Bath as a hydro to rival other British and Continental towns, where ailing Victorians would come to "take the waters". Matlock remains a prominent tourist resort and some of its glorious spa buildings have been beautifully refurbished.

MATLOCK BATH The photograph (right) is taken high above the Derwent and shows the Pump Room and the Matlock Pavilion, which date from 1910. Up river from Matlock Bath, the Derwent is sufficiently rapid to attract canoeing enthusiasts. By the time it reaches the town it has become much calmer, allowing for the hire of pleasure boats. The town's setting is distinctly Alpine, with steep and wooded valleys which create a picturesque scene. The similarity to the Alps was not lost on the Victorians who built the railway station at Matlock Bath in 1849 in the style of a Swiss chalet. In its heyday as a spa, both sides of the gorge were packed with hotels. The domed Royal Pavilion (right) at the centre of the spa complex at Matlock Bath was constructed in 1910. It contained a theatre, a large ballroom and an adjoining pump room to the right of the main building. The Pavilion has now found a new life as the Peak District Mining Museum. The museum offers a glimpse into the life of a leadminer and has climbing shafts, hazard tunnels and working models of a typical leadmine. The wooded hillside (above) rises above the busy north parade at Matlock Bath.

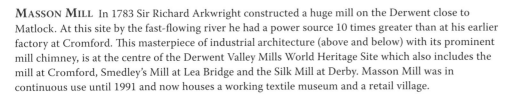

MASSON MILL In 1783 Sir Richard Arkwright constructed a huge mill on the Derwent close to Matlock. At this site by the fast-flowing river he had a power source 10 times greater than at his earlier factory at Cromford. This masterpiece of industrial architecture (above and below) with its prominent mill chimney, is at the centre of the Derwent Valley Mills World Heritage Site which also includes the mill at Cromford, Smedley's Mill at Lea Bridge and the Silk Mill at Derby. Masson Mill was in continuous use until 1991 and now houses a working textile museum and a retail village.

CROMFORD This town (left and right) is sometimes called "the cradle of the Industrial Revolution", thanks to the legacy of Richard Arkwright, the famous mill-owner who built the first successful water mill here in 1771. Before the arrival of Arkwright, Cromford was little more than a small hamlet.

BLACK ROCK An outcrop of gritstone sculpted by the wind and rain, Black Rock (below) hangs high above the historic town of Cromford with Cromford Moor behind and the High Peak Trail passing just below. It is a spectacular situation with splendid views of the Derwent Valley to the north and the more populated area around Wirksworth to the south-west. Black Rock is a popular venue for rock-climbing.

Dovedale

At the the heart of the White Peak, this dramatic limestone ravine is famous for its stunning scenery.

Steep-sided valleys carved from exposed limestone create the startling and colourful landscape of the South Peaks. The area is bounded to the west by the river Dove and to the east by the river Derwent. Adding a special charm to the landscape is the river Wye which runs diagonally from north-west to south-east through its centre. Many hilltops are the sites of ancient burial mounds; their rounded shapes and tumbledown cairns can be seen throughout the White Peak. Caves and dry river valleys are a common feature of the area.

DOVEDALE The river Dove rises on the southern side of Axe Edge and flows southwards to the boundary of the Peak District. The picturesque three-mile ravine between Milldale and Bunster Hill is owned by the National Trust. Along this section the limestone rocks on either side of the river resemble giant pieces of uplifted coral; the classic example are the superb crags of Tissington Spires.

One of the most popular walks is from the village of Ilam along the banks of the river where first Bunster Hill and then Thorpe Cloud stand guard over the entrance to the dale. Close by is the Izaak Walton Hotel, named after the author of *The Compleat Angler* who immortalised Dovedale. The stepping stones at the entrance to the dale are very popular with walkers.

54

THORPE CLOUD HILL The conical summit of Thorpe Cloud Hill (above) is one of the most distinctive sights in Dovedale. The peak towers above the village of Thorpe.

ILAM Visitors to Dovedale usually call at the pretty village of Ilam at the lower end of the river Manifold. The distinctive appearance of Ilam is due to the industrialist Jesse Watts-Russell. After the village was moved from its original position near Ilam Hall he rebuilt most of the cottages in the 1820s in a distinctive Alpine style. This explains the great distance between the village and Holy Cross church (far left). To the rear of the church is the Chantry Chapel. Part of the Victorian Gothic mansion of Ilam Hall (left) was demolished in the 1920s, before Sir Robert McDougall bought the estate and donated it to the National Trust in 1934. A walk through Ilam Park takes visitors past the Pepperpot (right) an ornate dovecote.

ASHBOURNE Situated at the southern tip of Derbyshire, near the Staffordshire border, Ashbourne is an attractive market town with many visitor attractions. The splendid stone building (far right) in Church Street housed the original Queen Elizabeth Grammar School established in 1585. The church of St Oswald (right) was described by the author George Eliot as "the finest mere parish church in the kingdom". Its spire is regarded as one of the grandest sights in Derbyshire.

At Ashbourne on December 3rd 1745, Charles Edward Stuart declared his father James King of England, Wales and Scotland.

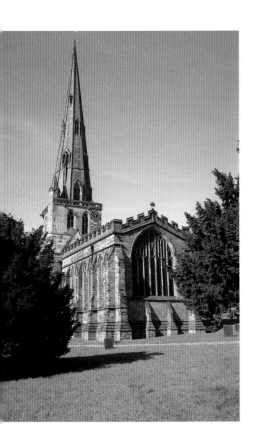

ASHBOURNE HISTORY In 1745, having defeated the British at Prestonpans, Charles Edward Stuart, commonly known as Bonnie Prince Charlie, advanced to Derby. While camped at Ashbourne in December 1745, he declared James, his father, king of England, Wales and Scotland; a plaque in the marketplace commemorates this event. Ashbourne is famous, or notorious, for the annual Royal Shrovetide football game, played on Shrove Tuesday and Ash Wednesday; it often resembles a re-enactment of the Civil War rather than a sporting event. The game is contested by two teams: those born on the north side of the river Henmore versus those born on the south side.

BUNSTER HILL

Between Bunster Hill and Thorpe Cloud the river Dove moves from Dovedale into Lin Dale, marked in the valley bottom by a set of stepping stones over the river. In the photograph below, Bunster Hill is on the left and Thorpe Cloud on the right with the wooded river ravine running between them.

South Peak Villages

The pretty villages of the White Peaks are mostly constructed from limestone – which gives the area a very distinctive appearance.

PARWICH This attractive village, situated on the high hills north of Ashbourne, is close to Dovedale and benefits from its location off the beaten track. In the centre of the village stands the Dam, once a sheep dip but now home to the village ducks, and close by the 17th century Sycamore Inn. The church of St Peter (above) appears to be Norman but is in fact Victorian and was built in 1873. Next to the church gate stands a beautiful limestone Celtic cross which serves as the village war memorial and honours the memory of those who fought and died in the two world wars. Above the village, Parwich Moor is home to many Bronze Age stone circles.

ALSTONEFIELD Located between Dovedale and the Manifold valley, Alstonefield (above and below) was an important market town until it was overtaken by nearby Ashbourne. Situated on the river Dove, the village contains many interesting old buildings, including an ancient tithe barn sited behind the 16th-century rectory. The church of St Peter has a doorway and chancel arch which dates back to Norman times; the church contains the pew of the Cotton family who were responsible for inviting Izaak Walton to Dovedale. Next to the village green is The George, a former coaching inn and behind it is the site of the once thriving wool market. Alstonefield is the home of the Hope House Costume Museum which contains a large collection of outfits dating back to the 18th century.

HARTINGTON North of Alstonefield, along the Dove valley, lies historic Hartington. This pretty settlement contains all the elements necessary for a picturesque village – a marketplace, village green, duckpond, 17th century hall, fine old church and limestone cottages. The parish church of St Giles (above) towers over the village and has a splendid Perpendicular tower. Hartington Hall (left) is a magnificent 17th-century Tudor manor house where Bonnie Prince Charlie once spent a night. Built in 1611 for Thomas Bateman it remained in the Bateman family for centuries until it was sold to the Youth Hostels Association in 1948.

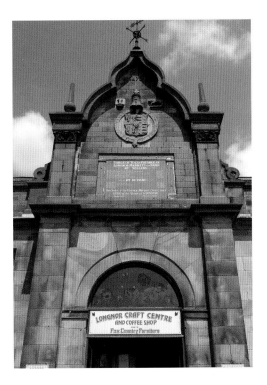

LONGNOR On the north bank of the river Manifold, just over the border in Staffordshire, the quaint village of Longnor has become famous as the setting for the television series *Peak Practice*. The cobbled market square, and the network of lanes that wind around the village, give Longnor a character all of its own. The church of St Bartholomew (right) contains the tomb of William Billinge who was born in a local cornfield in 1679 and lived until the age of 112. The old Victorian market hall (left), which stands at the head of the village square, dates from 1873 and displays a list of tariffs for making sales above the entrance.

BALLIDON This lonely hamlet (above and below) five miles north of Ashourne, was once a thriving settlement. All that remains now are some farms gathered near a large limestone quarry and a tiny, isolated chapel, Ballidon All Saints, which stands in a field surrounded by old farm buildings. Earthworks and enclosures in the fields surrounding the settlement show evidence of agricultural life in the Middle Ages. To the east are the remains of the Roman road which ran from Little Chester to Buxton. Nearby are a large number of chambered tombs and prehistoric burial sites including a Bronze Age and Roman barrow to the west of Green Low.

BRASSINGTON Located at the south-eastern corner of the Peak District, between Wirksworth and Ashbourne, this picturesque village was once a thriving centre for the local leadmining industry. The village is situated on a limestone plateau 800ft (240m) above sea level and the surrounding area is marked by the tell-tale hillocks and mounds of hundreds of long-since abandoned mines. Most of the cottages in the village are constructed from the local limestone and some date back to the 17th and 18th centuries. One of the oldest, inappropriately named the Tudor House, dates from 1615. Close to the village are the strange formations of Rainster Rocks, the site of a Roman settlement.

TISSINGTON Five miles north of Ashbourne, the attractive estate village of Tissington grew up around Tissington Hall, the home of the FitzHerbert family for over 400 years. Entry to the village from the main road is through a set of ornate gates. The magnificent Jacobean Tissington Hall (below) was built by Francis FitzHerbert in 1609. The hall and the estate have been enlarged many times over the centuries by his descendants. Other buildings of interest in the village include the Old School House (bottom right) which is now a kindergarten.

The Roaches

One of the most famous of the western Peak's millstone grit edges, the Roaches are popular with rock climbers.

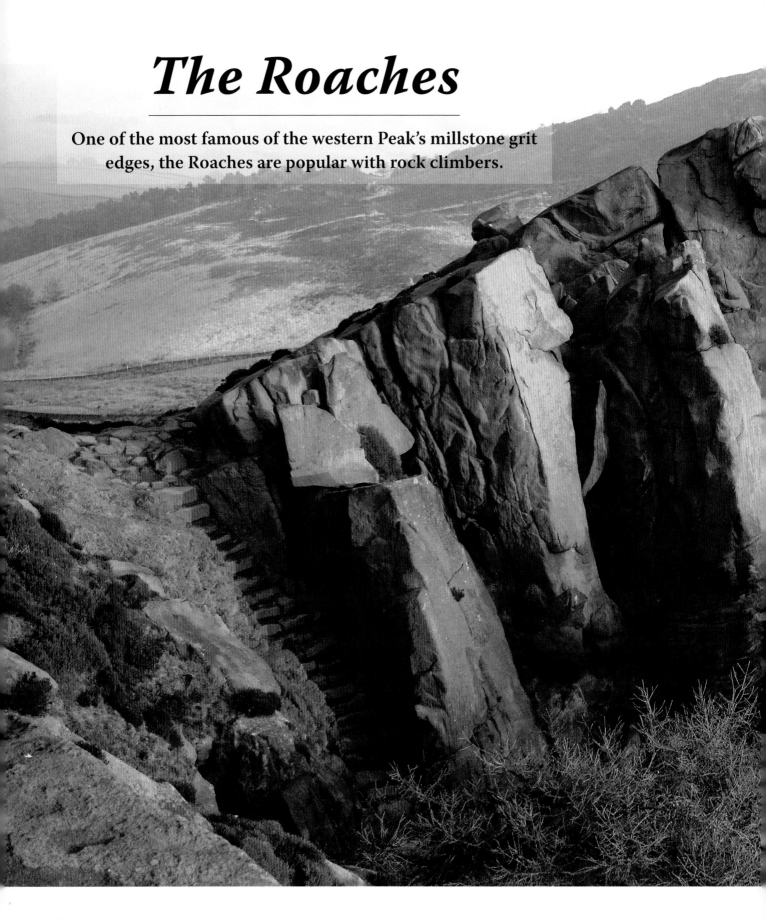

CLIMBER'S PARADISE The weirdly-shaped rocks of the Roaches provide a challenge to climbers; some of the cliff-routes have been given colourful names including "Saul's Crack", "the Valkyrie" and "the Mangler". On reaching the summit climbers are rewarded with spectacular views of Tittesworth Reservoir and the town of Leek in neighbouring Staffordshire. At the southern foot of the cliffs a climber's hut called Rockall Cottage has been built into the rockface. It has long been one of the area's main attractions, leading visitors to wonder at its precarious location beneath the overhanging gritstone rockface behind. The cottage is now a memorial to Don Whillans (1933-1985), the famous climber who pioneered many routes in this area.

HEN CLOUD The name "the
Roaches" is thought to derive from
les roches, the French for "the rocks".
The Roaches Estate, which extends
over 1,000 acres, was absorbed into
the Peak District national park in
1979. Hen Cloud (above) is a
separate, southern extremity of the
Roaches rising from the surrounding
moor to 1,555ft (410m) above sea
level. Hen Cloud overlooks the
village of Upper Hulme, a hamlet
clustered around a disused mill on
the upper reaches of the river
Churnet. The "fingerstone", right,
which resembles a giant hand
pointing heavenwards, is part of the
Ramshaw Rocks which lie between
the two farming hamlets of Upper
and Lower Elkstone.

WINDGATHER ROCKS Part of the escarpment which includes Shining Tor and Goyt's Bridge, Windgather Rocks (above) is a gritstone crag on the Derbyshire-Cheshire border north-east of Macclesfield. Popular with trainee rock-climbers, a circular walk from the famous Cat & Fiddle pub takes in all the best features of the escarpment. There are excellent views across the Cheshire Plain and the radio telescope at Jodrell Bank can often be seen. From Windgather Rocks it is possible to walk down to the Fernilee Reservoir and then on to Fernilee Dam, along the edge of a forest path. The name "Windgather" derives from the Victorian mania for christening every outcrop and cave they came across; most walkers find that this poetic name is particularly appropriate!

THE GOYT VALLEY The green pastures of the beautiful Goyt valley are broken up by a network of drystone walls, undulating hills and verdant forests. The valley bottoms are studded with reservoirs such as Fernilee and Errwood which are fed by the river Goyt. The river rises near the Cat & Fiddle and drains off Axe Moor. Fernilee was opened in 1938 and Errwood in 1967. Just to the west is the Lamaload Reservoir, fed by the river Dean with its impressive high concrete dam completed in 1964. There are wonderful views from the nearby Tegg's Nose summit across Nose and Bottoms, two of the smaller reservoirs.

WILDBOARCLOUGH This fine building at Wildboarclough, south-east of the Maccles-field Forest, was once the largest post office in England. It had previously served as the administration block for the carpet mill in the village. A few miles north-east of Wild-boarclough, on the Macclesfield to Buxton road, the historic Cat & Fiddle stands over 1,690ft (515m) above sea level. It is reputed to be the second highest pub in Britain and

is a favourite with walkers and motorcyclists. Visitors only have to step outside to enjoy spectacular views across the Cheshire Plain. The ancient Macclesfield to Buxton turnpike once ran behind the pub. Undecorated and austere, Jenkin Chapel – whose true name is the church of St John the Evangelist – stands within a bleak landscape close to Goyt's Bridge and Shining Tor, north-east of the Lamaload Reservoir. The church (right) stands beside one of the traditional "saltways", old packhorse routes used to transport Cheshire salt into Lancashire and Derbyshire. In 1733 the church was dedi-cated to St John the Baptist, but its name was changed to St John the Evangelist when it was consecrated in 1894. Its local name is thought to derive from that of a fiery Welsh drover who used to preach beside a nearby cross.

Castleton and Mam Tor

Unofficial capital of the central Peaks, this pretty town is close to Peveril castle and the looming ridge of Mam Tor.

Built in 1080 by William Peverel, one of William the Conqueror's most trusted allies and reputed to be his illegitimate son, Peveril Castle is perched above Cavedale, overlooking Castleton. The castle defended the royal hunting grounds and also the local lead-mining industry; the sheer sides of Cavedale helped make it impregnable. In the 1170s Henry II built the keep. By Tudor times the castle was too uncomfortable and went into decline, although the keep continued to be used as a courthouse. From Peveril there are breathtaking views over the surrounding countryside towards Mam Tor and north over the fields around Castleton towards the distant Lose Hill.

CASTLETON Situated at the western end of the broad Hope valley, where the dark gritstone Peaks of the north give way to the white limestone Peaks of the south, this picturesque village is one of the most popular destinations in the Peak District. It is surrounded on three sides by the looming hills of Mam Tor, Hollins Cross and Lose Hill. From the west the road runs through Winnats Pass, a dramatic narrow limestone gorge which for centuries was a packhorse route between Sheffield and Cheshire. Close by are Peveril castle and the four show caverns of Speedwell, Blue John, Treak Cliff and Peak Cavern – the source of the small river known as Peakshole Water which winds its way through the oldest part of the village and eventually joins the river Noe. Castleton was laid out as a planned village on a grid pattern towards the end of the 12th century. The mainly 17th century church of St Edmund was heavily restored in 1837 but the arch dates from the Norman period.

CASTLETON SIGHTS Other signs of the Norman era still remain – across the road by the Bull's Head Inn you can see a section of the Town Ditch – a defensive earthwork built around the village. Castleton's square is surrounded by fine old houses and cottages including a youth hostel and The George Inn. The unusual Celtic cross on the green is the village war memorial.

MAM TOR Known as the "Mother Mountain" because of its softly rounded contours, Mam Tor is formed from an unstable mix of sandstone and shale. The entire hill is gradually slipping into the valley giving the peak its other name of the "shivering mountain". The old main road from Manchester to Sheffield was forced to close in 1979 due to this slippage. The view above is of the eastern exposed face of the hill. The track (right and far right) that connects the 1700ft (518m) summit to that of Lose Hill to the north is now paved. It forms a route along which a seemingly endless succession of walkers, young and old, make their way.

LOSE HILL From Castleton there is an enjoyable 6.5 mile (10km) walk that takes in Lose Hill and Winnats Pass. Walkers cross the Hope Valley to the gradually swelling shape of Lose Hill, which rises to 1560ft (476m). At the summit a stone waymarker (right) gives information about the surrounding scenery. The route south-west traverses Barker Bank and there are breathtaking views of Mam Tor (above). The walk goes full circle taking in Peveril Castle on the way and returning weary walkers to Castleton in time for tea.

WINNATS PASS A zig-zag path brings the walker up onto the spectacular limestone gorge which overlooks Winnats Pass (above). This is the only route for vehicles out of the head of the Hope Valley. The road climbs to 1300ft (396m) through a spectacular narrow gorge hemmed in by high limestone cliffs on either side. This lonely spot is the source of many stories and local legends. At the lower end of the pass is Speedwell Cavern. The main workings and the "bottomless pit" can only be approached by boat along a narrow flooded tunnel – the same journey taken by the original miners.

Northern Peak Villages

Set amongst wild moorland, the villages of the northern Peak District are a magnet for fell-walkers and visitors who want to get off the beaten track.

Nestling beneath the cliffs of Bamford Edge, the village of Bamford occupies an attractive position on the banks of the river Derwent close to the dams of the Upper Derwent valley. The 18th century mill (above) was built by the Manchester cotton magnate H. Cameron Moore using gritstone from Bamford Edge. The mill closed down in the 1960s and now houses modern apartments. The mill wheel survives, and the adjoining mill pool (right) is one of the prettiest spots along the Derwent. The church of St John the Baptist (left) has an interesting design featuring a slim tower and a tall sharp spire. Bamford lies on the old Sheffield to Manchester turnpike, and the Mytham bridge tollgate – just below the station – has recently been refurbished.

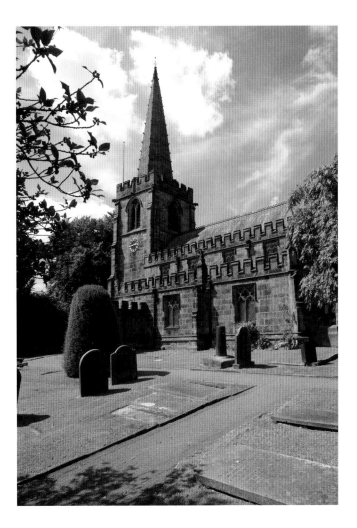

HATHERSAGE On the banks of the river Derwent, 10 miles west of Sheffield, Hathersage is a large gritstone village surrounded by wild moorland. The village is now popular with walkers and climbers but at one time this area was an industrial hub. In the mid 18th century Hathersage was famous for its brass buttons and was the centre of the wire, pin and needle industry. In the early years of the 20th century Hathersage declined as Sheffield developed and became the world centre of the steel trade. The author Charlotte Brontë stayed at the vicarage in 1845 while writing *Jane Eyre*. Henry, the brother of her friend Ellen Nussey, was the vicar of the parish church of St Michael and All Angels at the time. Charlotte Brontë was inspired by brass rubbings in the church dedicated to the local Eyre family of Padley, and took their family name for the heroine of her famous novel. The church of St Michael and All Angels (left) stands on a knoll above the village.

HOPE The village of Hope is sited at the confluence of Peakshole Water and the river Noe, below Win Hill and Lose Hill.
Hope is justly famous for the craftsmanship and ingenuity of its annual well-dressings (far right) each July. These decorations are made by covering large boards with damp clay and then attaching petals, bark and other natural objects to make an attractive picture.

The figure of the climber (right) scaling the west face of Old Hall Cottage represents the Yorkshire mountaineer Alan Hinkes, who in 2005 completed ascents of all 14 of the world's 8000m peaks, the first Briton to achieve this feat. The fine parish church of St Peter has a squat square tower topped off by a spire. Inside there are two stone coffin lids bearing the motifs of royal huntsmen.

GLOSSOP There are two Glossops – the bustling market town on the main A57 road from Manchester to Sheffield, and Old Glossop, a collection of older buildings gathered round the parish church. Situated in the far north-west of Derbyshire, just outside the boundaries of the Peak District National Park, Glossop was settled by the Romans in the first century AD, and a Roman road known as Doctor's Gate leads from Old Glossop to the slopes of Bleaklow, high up on the Snake Pass. The new town was mostly built in the 19th century, centred around the town hall, and originally named Howard Town, before acquiring the name Glossop from the ancient village settlement now known as Old Glossop. Old Glossop features many 17th and 18th century cottages clustered around the Norman church, and standing opposite is a fine old 13th century carved stone cross, although the top is a 20th century addition, marking the coronation of George V in 1910. The village expanded rapidly during the 16th and 17th centuries, as the wool and cotton industries grew; the cottages would have been occupied by weavers.

CHAPEL-EN-LE-FRITH The busy market town of Chapel-en-le-Frith stands 776ft (237m) above sea level between Stockport and Buxton. Its attractive cobbled marketplace contains stocks dating back to the Cromwellian period, together with a market cross. Church Brow (below) is a steep, cobbled street leading down from Market Street to the High Street, lined with quaint stone cottages.

The Peak Forest Tramway once passed through the town and linked Bugsworth Canal Basin, at the head of the Peak Forest Canal, to the limestone quarries at Dove Holes Dale. The tramway was a busy network of horse-drawn wagons running on rails. Today the tramway is an historic trail which is steeped in the history of limestone and the factories associated with its production.

TRADITIONS AND FESTIVALS The name Chapel-en-le-Frith means "chapel in the forest clearing" and derives from the French. The settlement was established as a hunting lodge in the 12th century in what was then a densely-forested area. The first chapel, built at the highest point in the town, has since been replaced by the church of St Thomas Becket. The churchyard contains the graves of many soldiers in the Scottish army who marched south in support of the Stuart king, Charles I, in 1648. Every July Chapel-en-le-Frith hosts a carnival and well-dressing takes place in five different locations, including Nanny's Well on Crossings Road and the Town's Well on the forecourt of the Town Hall. A highlight of the carnival is the Scarecrow Festival in which lifelike figures are placed around the town.

Sheffield in the Peak

The north-east corner of the Peak District is home to Sheffield in the Peak – an area of attractive reservoirs bordering the city of Sheffield.

Together with the Derwent and Howden, the Ladybower is one of three reservoirs built in the Upper Derwent valley to supply water to Sheffield, Derby, Nottingham and Leicester. Built between 1935 and 1943 it submerged the villages of Derwent and Ashopton. Much of the stone used to reinforce the dam came from houses in Derwent; the Derwent pumphouse is pictured (left). The view (right) looks south-east down the eastern spur of Ladybower from the Snake Pass – the highest part of the A57 road between Sheffield and Manchester, home to Snake Pass Inn.

LADYBOWER Looking south down the upper spur of the Ladybower (left), this photograph was taken from a parking spot just north of the war memorial marking the practice runs of the Dambusters before their daring wartime raids on the Möhne, Sorpe and Eder dams in the Ruhr. The beautiful placid waters of the three reservoirs and the fact that they lie within easy reach of Sheffield, help to make this one of the Peak District's most popular spots. The area attracts large numbers of cyclists and walkers who enjoy meandering along the gentle waterside paths.

BRADFIELD Lying 10 miles to the north-west of Sheffield this Peak village is divided into Low Bradfield and High Bradfield. High Bradfield has extensive views across Bradfield towards Derwent Edge. Low Bradfield, which lies just to the south-west but at considerably lower altitude, was largely destroyed in the Great Sheffield Flood of 1864. This was caused when the dam wall of Dale Dyke Dam, a recently built reservoir, broke and millions of gallons of water surged down the Loxley valley towards Mallin Bridge and Hillsborough. More than 240 people were drowned, over 400 houses destroyed and 15 stone bridges swept away. The church of St Nicholas (above) which stood close to the dam survived remarkably unscathed. Three headstones in the graveyard commemorate victims of the flood. By the main gate is an irregular-shaped watch house (above) built to protect the churchyard from grave robbers who would steal corpses for medical studies. Opposite the Old Horns Inn stands the remains of the administrative block of the old workhouse (right) built in 1769 to house the poor of the parish and the paupers' graveyard.

Kinder Scout

This desolate stretch of high moorland contains the Peak District's highest spot.

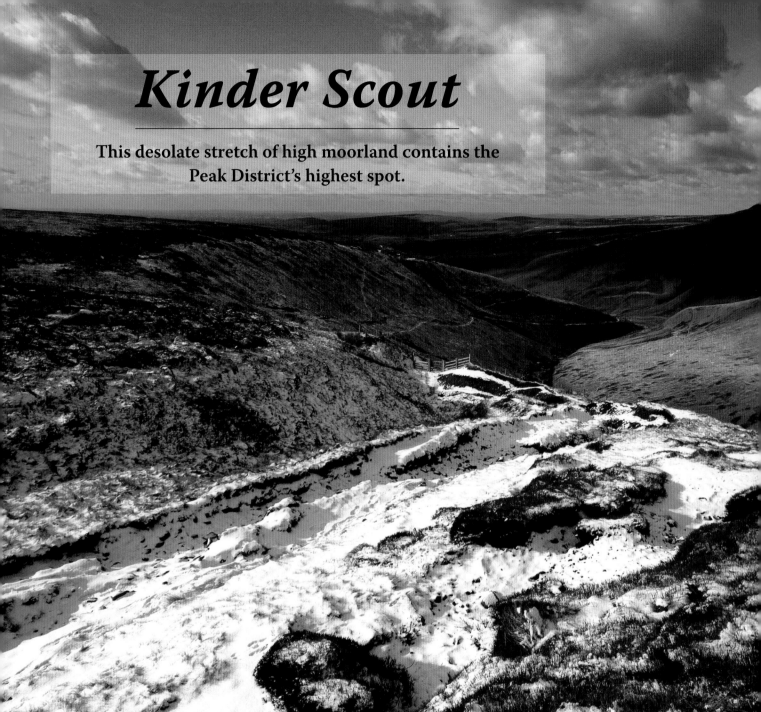

The windswept 15-mile wide plateau of Kinder Scout is a desolate mix of wind and ice-shattered boulders, peat bogs and deep trenches called "groughs". Located midway between Manchester and Sheffield, it is a great attraction for walkers and lovers of challenging upland terrain. The name Kinder Scout derives from the Saxon words for "water over the edge" and nowhere is this more appropriate than at Kinder Downfall (above right) on its north-western edge where much of the

plateau's water gathers to drop 98ft (30m) on to the land below. At times of drought this is little more than a trickle but in wet weather a spectacular waterfall is formed often blown skyward by high winds. In wintry conditions the water can freeze creating a ribbon of silver against the darker slopes of the surrounding moorland. The photograph (above) is of Doctor's Gate – a bleak spot which by legend is named after John Talbot, vicar of Glossop, who built this track to link Sheffield and Glossop.

AIRCRAFT GRAVEYARD Kinder has been the site of many plane disasters, some occurring during the Second World War when bombers returning from night raids would become lost over the dark landscape. The skeletal remains (right) show the wreckage of a plane emerging from the peat bog.

OVER OWLER AND HIGGER TOR The surreal, almost lunar landscapes of Over Owler Tor (below) and Higger Tor (right), where rounded rocks perch precariously on top of one another, are located south-east of Hathersage and the Derwent valley. These are thought to have been the inspiration for parts of Charlotte Brontë's famous novel *Jane Eyre*. Just beyond Higger Tor stands the remarkable escarpment hillfort of Carl Wark. The fort utilised the sheer cliffs on three sides to provide an easily defended position. The origins of this hillfort are still contested – it could possibly date from the Iron Age.

HAYFIELD Overlooked by the bulk of Kinder Scout, Hayfield sits on a Roman road and old packhorse route between Yorkshire and Cheshire. The many three-storey weavers' cottages in the village were built when Hayfield was a centre for cotton and wool-spinning. The industry went into decline in the mid 19th century and the village only began to recover in the 20th century when it became one of the starting points for visitors who wished to climb Kinder Scout. In 1932 this was the site of the "Mass Trespass" when hundreds of ramblers set out from Bowden Bridge Quarry onto Kinder Scout to challenge the authority of landowners who restricted access to the open moorland. After holding a meeting the marchers continued up to Ashop Head; on their return to Hayfield a number of them were arrested and five were subsequently gaoled. The actions of the "mass trespassers" paved the way for the formation of Britain's national parks and the later "right to roam" legislation.

EDALE The little village of Edale marks the start of the Pennine Way, Britain's first long-distance footpath which continues for 250 miles northwards. The path joins the Pennine Ridge, passes through the Yorkshire Dales, continues up into Northumberland and eventually ends at Kirk Yetholm in the Scottish Borders. It takes a fit walker about 16 days to complete the journey. By tradition, before embarking on the trek north, walkers call in at the Old Nag's Head (left). From Edale the Pennine Way winds through Grindsbrook Clough before climbing to Kinder Scout which, at 2088ft (636m), is the highest point in Derbyshire. Large parts of the Pennine Way are paved with flagstones because of their dangerous bogs. Edale – a collection of the six small hamlets of Edale, Netherbooth, Ollerbooth, Upper Booth, Barber Booth and Grindsbrook Booth – became a centre for walking when the railway which linked Manchester to Sheffield arrived in 1894.

STANAGE EDGE Lying on the western moors with views over the Derwent valley, Stanage (literally "stone edge") is the largest and most impressive of the Peaks' gritstone edges and is visible from far down in the Hope valley. The entire edge is approximately 3.5 miles long from its northern tip to the southern point near the Cowper Stone. The highest point is High Neb which reaches a height of 1502ft (458m). In winter much of Stanage Edge is often snowbound. It is an ideal spot for climbing, since some of the rockfaces reach a height of 82ft (25m). The more challenging sections have been given fanciful names such as Marble Wall, the Tower, Black Hawk and Robin Hood's Cave. Climbs were made here as early as the 1890s; in this period, and well into the early 20th century, climbers often had to bribe local gamekeepers in order to gain access to the high ground. A paved packhorse route ran along the top of the edge and its route can still be traced.

First published in 2010 by Myriad Books Limited
35 Bishopsthorpe Road
London SE26 4PA

Photographs and text copyright © 2010 Simon Kirwan

Simon Kirwan has asserted his right under the Copyright, Designs and Patents Act, 1988, to be identified as the author of this work. All rights reserved. No part of this publication may be reproduced, stored in a retrieval system or transmitted in any form or by any means, electronic, mechanical, photocopying, recording or otherwise without the prior permission of the copyright owners.

ISBN   1 84746 351 7
EAN 978 1 84746 351 7

Designed by Jerry Goldie Graphic Design

Printed in China